Kid Pick!

Title: _____

Author: _____ 012209

Picked by: _____

Why I love this book:

_____

_____

_____

The Korean
Americans

TAMRA ORR

MAJOR AMERICAN IMMIGRATION

MASON CREST PUBLISHERS • PHILADELPHIA

Pedestrians walk through a street filled with signs in Seoul, South Korea. Seoul is one of the most densely populated cities in the world, with an average of 41,000 people per square mile.

The Korean Americans

TAMRA ORR

MAJOR AMERICAN IMMIGRATION

MASON CREST PUBLISHERS • PHILADELPHIA

Mason Crest Publishers
370 Reed Road
Broomall PA 19008
www.masoncrest.com

First printing

1 3 5 7 9 8 6 4 2

Library of Congress Cataloging-in-Publication Data

Orr, Tamra.
  The Korean Americans / Tamra Orr.
      p. cm. — (Major American immigration)
  Includes index.
  ISBN 978-1-4222-0612-6 (hardcover)
  ISBN 978-1-4222-0679-9 (pbk.)
  1. Korean Americans—History--Juvenile literature. 2. Korean
Americans—Social conditions—Juvenile literature. 3. Immigrants—
United States—History—Juvenile literature. 4. United States—
Emigration and immigration—Juvenile literature. 5. Korea—
Emigration and immigration—Juvenile literature. I. Title.
  E184.K6O773 2008
  973'.04957—dc22
                                                    2008026019

Table of Contents

MAJOR AMERICAN IMMIGRATION

America's Ethnic Heritage

Barry Moreno, librarian
Statue of Liberty/
Ellis Island National Monument

Ethnic diversity is one of the most striking characteristics of the American identity. In the United States the Bureau of the Census officially recognizes 122 different ethnic groups. North America's population had grown by leaps and bounds, starting with the American Indian tribes and nations—the continent's original people—and increasing with the arrival of the European colonial migrants who came to these shores during the 16th and 17th centuries. Since then, millions of immigrants have come to America from every corner of the world.

But the passage of generations and the great distance of America from the "Old World"—Europe, Africa, and Asia—has in some cases separated immigrant peoples from their roots. The struggle to succeed in America made it easy to forget past traditions. Further, the American spirit of freedom, individualism, and equality gave Americans a perspective quite different from the view of life shared by residents of the Old World.

Immigrants of the 19th and 20th centuries recognized this at once. Many tried to "Americanize" themselves by tossing away their peasant clothes and dressing American-style even before reaching their new homes in the cities or the countryside of America. It was not so easy to become part of America's culture, however. For many immigrants, learning English was quite a hurdle. In fact, most older immigrants clung to the old ways, preferring to speak their native languages and follow their familiar customs and traditions. This was easy to do when ethnic neighborhoods abounded in large North American cities like New York, Montreal, Philadelphia, Chicago, Toronto, Boston, Cleveland, St. Louis, New Orleans and San Francisco. In rural areas, farm families—many of them Scandinavian, German, or Czech—established their own tightly knit communities. Thus foreign languages and dialects, religious beliefs, Old World customs, and certain class distinctions flourished.

The most striking changes occurred among the children of immigrants, whose hopes and dreams were different from those of their parents. They began breaking away from the Old World customs, perhaps as a reaction to the embarrassment of being labeled "foreigner." They badly wanted to be Americans, and assimilated more easily than their parents and grandparents. They learned to speak English without a foreign accent, to dress and act like other Americans. The assimilation of the children of immigrants was encouraged by social contact—games, schools, jobs, and military service—which further broke down the barriers between immigrant groups and hastened the process of Americanization. Along the way, many family traditions were lost or abandoned.

Today, the pride that Americans have in their ethnic roots is one of the abiding strengths of both the United States and Canada. It shows that the theory which called America a "melting pot" of the world's people was never really true. The thought that a single "American" would emerge from the combination of these peoples has never happened, for Americans have grown more reluctant than ever before to forget the struggles of their ethnic forefathers. The growth of cultural studies and genealogical research indicates that Americans are anxious not to entirely lose this identity, whether it is English, French, Chinese, African, Mexican, or some other group. There is an interest in tracing back the family line as far as records or memory will take them. In a sense, this has made Americans a divided people; proud to be Americans, but proud also of their ethnic roots.

As a result, many Americans have welcomed a new identity, that of the hyphenated American. This unique description has grown in usage over the years and continues to grow as more Americans recognize the importance of family heritage. In the end, this is an appreciation of America's great cultural heritage and its richness of its variety.

1 Coming to America

Nin Sun Cha was the oldest child and the only daughter of her family. When she took a job as a clerk in a Korean department store, she never realized that she was actually opening the door to an all-new and different way of life.

"One day," she says, "I was helping a young American man pick a birthday present for his mother and we began talking. He was stationed in South Korea and soon after that, we got married." She adds, "I knew I would be moving to America with him. It was very hard."

Imagine leaving your entire family, home, and way of life behind to go to another country thousands of miles away! Would you be frightened? Sun Cha was.

Shoppers crowd a busy market street in Seoul. The city is Korea's main industrial center, as well as a hub of banking and education. Seoul remains the capital of South Korea; it is relatively close to the border with North Korea.

"I was very scared," she says. "I didn't know very much English, I didn't know how to drive, and I'd never met my new family. My father would not speak to me after I told him I was leaving Korea, and my

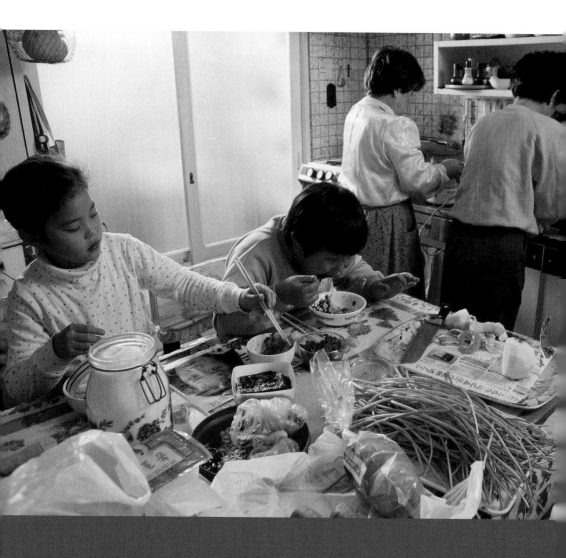

A Korean family prepares a meal in their
kitchen. Many Koreans still cook using
traditional ingredients, such as rice,
noodles, meats, tofu, and fresh vegetables.

mother, she took it very, very hard.

"I am pretty outgoing, though, and I love an adventure, so it was also exciting for me," she continued. "I knew that in America there would be opportunities for me to explore myself and who I am. In Korea, life just stops when you become a wife and mother. I knew that in the United States, I could do these things and still meet with friends and have a job. Here, a woman has choices!"

Do you think that you would go back to your homeland to visit your family? Many immigrants do just this, and so does Sun Cha. "I return home every five or six years," she says. "I stay for at least a month and visit my relatives. Korea has changed much since I was there, but I still like my life in the U.S. better." She adds, "I hope that one day I can get my family to come and visit me here. They think about it but they are frightened to do it. The entire country of Korea is about the same size as the state I live in. To get food, they just walk or bicycle to the market. They cannot imagine having to get into a car and drive 20 or 30 miles to a grocery store."

Sun Cha tries to share some of her Korean heritage with her two young sons. "I do a lot of Korean cooking," she says. "My boys love rice and will ask for it if I don't make it for a few days. I also make sure they take their shoes off at the front door of the house as I was taught to do and I am teaching them a few words of Korean here and there."

Helen Kim, a Korean woman who came to America with her family when she was only 12 years old, also speaks of how hard it

Have you ever heard of Confucius? He was a Chinese *philosopher* who lived from 551 to 479 B.C. Many Korean families followed some of his teachings and continue to do so even though they are now living in the United States. Some of the lessons that they believe in include:

- **Modesty:** Koreans feel that the way you act and talk should be modest. This means you don't make eye contact with people who are older than you, and you speak clearly, softly, and with respect.

- **Hierarchy:** Koreans believe that there is a distinct order of importance to things. For example, they think that older people are more important than younger and so deserve more honor. Calling an elder by his or her first name would be considered extremely rude, and when meeting, the younger person should always bow to the older first.

- **Dignity:** Koreans feel that they should always look dignified and strong, so they rarely smile at anyone they don't know very well, as that can indicate weakness.

- **House Rules:** Some Koreans do not allow shoes to be worn in the house or hats in any buildings.

A statue of Confucius, the revered Chinese sage and philosopher, stands in a temple. His teachings about moral conduct had great influence on Asia's history and culture.

- **Education:** An excellent education for children is extremely important to Koreans. In Korea, one of the biggest insults you can give someone is to say, "You are an uneducated person."

This map shows the relation between China, Japan, and North and South Korea. Korea has served historically as both a land bridge and a buffer between China and Japan. Korea itself is divided into the Communist north and the non-Communist south.

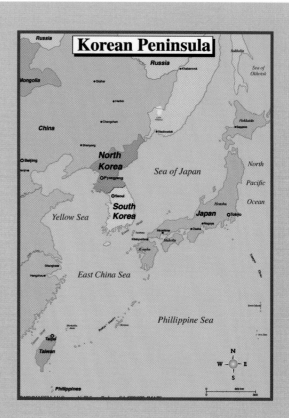

was to leave her family. "We said our goodbyes to Grandmother, who had lived with us, and to many aunts, uncles, cousins, and friends who had been a part of our lives. As the bus pulled away from the terminal to the runway, we bowed and cried and held in our memories the vanishing sight of Grandmother shaking her white handkerchief."

Like Sun Cha, Helen was excited about coming to a new land. "My older sister, my younger sisters, and I couldn't wait to get to America. To us, America was the magical land of Disney World,

Charms candies, Hershey's chocolates, and the Sears catalog. The American movie *Parent Trap* and…television shows…promised us that we were going to a country where everything was plentiful, orderly, and fun."

Leaving everything they know and going to live in a mysterious and foreign place is something that people all over the world have done for centuries. These adventurous people are often scared, worried, and homesick, but they are also determined to make a new—and often better—life for themselves. They are *immigrants*, and they are what help to make the United States a unique and special place. ✴

A teenaged Korean boy spends time with his family on their small farm in this photograph from the 1950s. Until the last half of the 20th century, the Koreans were a rural people. In 1925, less than 5 percent of the population lived in or near cities. Today, more than half of the 70 million people living in North and South Korea live in cities.

2 The First Wave (1900-1953)

The Japanese laborers were through. They had been working on Hawaii's sugar and pineapple plantations for years and they wanted more money and better working conditions. It was the start of a new century—the 20th century—and time to call a strike!

Horace N. Allen, the American minister to Korea, had just returned from a visit to Korea where he had acted as Emperor Kojong's personal doctor. He thought he had a wonderful solution to the problem of the angry workers. He began talking to the members of the Hawaiian Sugar Planters' Association (HSPA) and convinced them that the answer to their labor problems was not an increase in pay or any improvement in the conditions. Instead, the answer was bringing in a new group of workers who wouldn't complain—Koreans. Emperor Kojong agreed to let his people immigrate to other lands because of the terrible floods, droughts, and *famine* in his country, and so, in 1902, the first boat of Korean immigrants landed on American soil. Sailing on the U.S.S. *Gaelic* were 56 men, 21 women, and 25 children, all with hope in their hearts of a better life. These first Korean immigrants looked to the United States as a place to start over and also as a place where they could have freedom not available in their home country.

During the next three years, almost 8,000 other Koreans followed in their footsteps. Most of them were single young men who had once been soldiers, laborers, and peasants. Unfortunately, few of them found the success they had hoped for when they put their homes far behind them. Too quickly, they discovered why the Japanese workers had refused to work on the plantations. Hours were long—often up to 10 hours a day—and pay was low—less than $4 a week! The living conditions were awful, with everyone crowded together into large camps.

A Korean foreman, or *luna*, later wrote about his experiences. "I was in charge of 250 workers—200 men and 50 women," he wrote. "After receiving my assignment, I would take my group out to the fields and begin work at 6:00. We worked 10 hours a day in the blazing sun and had only a half hour for lunch…I had workers of all races in my group…We would quit work at 4:30 and walk wearily to the train that would take us back to camp. When we got back…we ate, washed, and went directly to bed. During the harvest season, we worked seven days a week."

Soon, some of these unhappy immigrants began to move on to other places. Around 1,000 of them went back home to Korea, while another 1,000 headed to the mainland and nearby San Francisco, California. There, they joined together to create several Korean temples and other organizations. The temple was a place they could go to talk, visit, and enjoy being around other Koreans, and they spent much of their free time there.

In 1905, the migration of Koreans to North America came to a sudden halt. Japan took complete control over all of Korea's affairs and put a stop to all immigration. While in the beginning it had seemed like the Japanese were there to help protect Korea, it soon became clear that they were actually there to take over and rule the country. By 1910, Japan totally controlled the country, destroying

Emperor Gojong ruled Korea from 1864 to 1907. He tried to maintain Korea's independence from Japan, but was forced to abdicate the throne in favor of his son, Sunjong. Three years later, Japan's government forced Sunjong to turn control of Korea over to Japan.

many of the old traditions that had been handed down from family to family for centuries. Koreans were horrified, and immigrants in the U.S. suddenly felt like *exiles* without a country to which they could return.

The only people that were leaving Korea during this time were "picture brides" and students. Since the majority of the early immigrants had been unmarried men, they were now ready to start families, but they only wanted to marry Korean women. Between 1910 and 1924, almost 1,000 women left Korea to come to the U.S. as new brides. Most of them went to Hawaii, but about 100 went directly to California. The Japanese were in control of that process, too. They played the role of matchmaker, putting together possible grooms with potential brides and exchanging their pictures by mail.

Many of the emigrants from Korea traveled to Hawaii, a group of islands that became a territory of the United States in 1900. There, they worked long hours on sugar and fruit plantations. From Hawaii, some immigrants eventually traveled to the mainland United States.

Hence, the term "picture bride." If both the man and the woman agreed to the marriage (all from one picture!), the Japanese would then perform the entire wedding ceremony in Korea—without a groom! The husband in the U.S. would, in turn, send money to ship his new bride to America and she would sail to him. It must have been frightening for these young women to leave their homes and go live with someone they knew nothing about other than what their husbands looked like.

Can you imagine traveling thousands of miles to go to school? That is exactly what about 500 Korean students did during this time. They wanted to study at different American universities and colleges. They were only allowed to stay in the country until they graduated, however, and then were sent right back home to Korea.

In 1924, the Oriental Exclusion Act was passed, which placed a **ban** on all Asian immigrants, except for the students. This law remained in place until 1965, so almost all Korean immigration was put on hold for 40 years. Throughout the 1930s, Korean immigrants continued to live in San Francisco and Los Angeles, California.

However, the world changed dramatically when World War II began. Japan's control of Korea ended with the war. In 1948 Korea became divided, with North Korea becoming a Communist state united with the Soviet Union, and South Korea joining with the U.S. Slowly, the number of immigrants from South Korea began to creep up again. The postwar economy offered them much stronger chances

The Korean language is quite different from English. It is primarily written in symbols rather than letters. Through a process called *Romanization*, however, you can see how some everyday words and phrases would look if they were written out using English letters:

Welcome..*Oso oseyo*

What's your name?.........................*Irumi muosim nigga*

Thank you ....*Kamsa hamnida*

Goodbye ....*Annyonghi kaseyo*

You're welcome ....*Ch' onmanyeo*

Members of a Congressional committee inspect the passports of Asian "picture brides" at the Angel Island Immigration Station in California. During the early years of the 20th century, some Korean immigrants who wished to get married and start families agreed to marry Korean women whom they had never met. Often, the groom was not present at the wedding ceremony, which was held at the bride's home in Korea. The groom then paid for his new wife to travel to the United States.

at better jobs, homes, and education, and little by little, they made the trip to the United States or Canada to grab these opportunities.

As the 1950s were ushered in, things changed even more—and television was one of the reasons. Suddenly, the lifestyles of Americans were being seen all over the world in different shows, and this made these "strange" American foreigners seem a lot less frightening to people in other countries.

An even stronger influence on how Koreans felt about Americans occurred on June 27, 1950, with the beginning of the Korean War. The United States quickly joined the South Koreans in an attempt to stop North Korea, a Communist state since 1946, and China from invading the south. For three long years, thousands of men and women fought in the Korean War, with neither side gaining much ground. In July 1953, an *armistice* was finally declared. During those years, Koreans often saw American soldiers with rare luxuries like gum, food, and cameras, and this made them even more certain that America must truly be the land of opportunity. Many South Koreans began to set their sights on this land far away.

KOREAN NAMES

In Korea, people usually have three names, just as in the United States. The family name, which is listed last here, comes first in Korea. The second name usually tells what generation or clan a person is from, and the last name is the personal name. How does your name sound in a different order? Would it feel strange to sign your name as Smith Douglas Kevin instead of Kevin Douglas Smith or as Brown Marie Susan instead of Susan Marie Brown? Another difference in Korea is that when the women marry, they keep their family name rather than changing it to their husband's, as many of the women in this country do.

There are only a few basic family names used in Korea. In the U.S., there are several common names, such as Smith, Jones, and Brown, but in Korea, over half of all the people are named Kim, Lee, or Park. The rest are usually named Chung, Cho, Choi, Yu, Yun, Kang, Han, Ko, Lim, Shin, or Oh.

THE KOREAN WAR

On the morning of June 25, 1950, North Korea launched a surprise invasion of its neighbor, South Korea. Tens of thousands of North Korean soldiers streamed across the 38th parallel of latitude, the border between the two nations, and quickly overwhelmed the South's armed forces. Within three days the South Korean capital, Seoul, had fallen.

In response to the aggression by Communist North Korea, which was supported by the Soviet Union, the United Nations called for its member countries to come to the aid of democratic South Korea. Eventually 16 nations, led by the United States, answered that call by sending troops. But in the early weeks of the fighting, it appeared that the North Koreans would win a rapid victory. By late July 1950, they controlled almost the entire Korean Peninsula. South Korean and American troops clung only to a small piece of land around the port city of Pusan.

In mid-September 1950, a U.S. Marine division landed behind North Korean lines at Inchon, southwest of Seoul. Within weeks the North

American paratroopers are dropped into Korea during a combat jump in 1951. The war claimed the lives of over 54,000 American soldiers.

Koreans had been pushed back to the 38th parallel.

Although North Korea announced that it would now be willing to accept its prewar border with the South, United Nations commanders decided to keep fighting. By late November the North Koreans had retreated to the Yalu River, near the border with the People's Republic of China. At that point the Communist Chinese decided to enter the fight, throwing some 300,000 troops at the U.N. front.

American Marines watch artillery fire in Korea. The Korean War ended with an armistice on July 27, 1953.

By the end of 1950, under the Chinese onslaught, U.N. troops had retreated to a line just south of the 38th parallel. Over the next few months, they counterattacked, moving the front north of that line. For the next two and a half years, the fighting, while bloody, did not dramatically change the amount of territory controlled by each side.

After months of frustrating negotiations, on July 27, 1953, a truce ending the fighting was finally signed. An official peace treaty has never been worked out, however, and today relations between North and South Korea remain tense.

More than 625,000 U.N. servicemen lost their lives in the Korean War, the vast majority of them from South Korea's armed forces. The number of North Korean and Chinese troops killed is not known, though it is believed to be higher.

The Second Wave (1952–1965)

After the Korean War finally ended, the largest group of Korean immigrants to come to the United States was the Korean wives and children of the servicemen who were coming home from the war, or who were stationed in South Korea to maintain the border with North Korea. Between 1950 and 1975, more than 28,000 Korean women and children came to America. Because of the war, Korea also had a lot of orphaned children. Families in the United States and Canada adopted over 6,000 of these children. Korean students also continued to travel to North America in search of a quality education. Over 10,000 came durng the late 1950s.

Korean immigrants were beginning to expand into more states. The two main areas they migrated to were around San Francisco and Los Angeles in California and the Queens and Bronx neighborhoods of New York City. They also headed to places like Seattle, Chicago, and even Vancouver, Canada.

A Korean woman and young boy participate in a parade celebrating the birthday of Siddhartha Guatama. Siddhartha, who lived about 2,500 years ago, was a Hindu prince. His teachings led to the creation of a new religion, Buddhism. Today, about 25 percent of Koreans are Buddhists.

Then, in the mid-1960s, the United States found itself with an unexpected *shortage* of doctors and other medical professionals. What could they do about it? In Korea, the majority of adults had college educations and degrees, many of which were in medicine. So many Koreans had medical degrees, in fact, that they couldn't find jobs anywhere in Korea. The United States saw this as an excellent solution to the problem, and it was decided to make special arrangements for these medical school graduates and their families to come to America to practice. Sometimes the country even paid for the airplane tickets to fly them here. Within 10 years, over 13,000 doctors, nurses, pharmacists, and dentists had been brought from Korea to the U.S. to work.

Il Soo Kim is a young man who came to the United States in 1965 at the age of 16 with the rest of his family. His father was a colonel in the Korean Armed Forces, and they all moved to Princeton, New Jersey. "I expected all Americans to be blonde and blue-eyed like Robert Redford," he says. "I also thought the buildings would be higher. The Lincoln Tunnel, though, was really impressive. My

A group of orphans line up at the Children's Protective Home at Pusan where they have been washed and shaved. The Korean War left about 60,000 orphans on the streets of South Korea in the 1950s. Many orphaned children were adopted by families in the United States or Canada.

A priest prepares for a ceremony in a Buddhist temple. Other religions practiced on the peninsula are Confucianism, Christianity, and Chondogyo, a religious system native to Korea that was created in the mid-19th century.

father was happy. We could develop freer. You can't study with a clear head if you're always on guard, afraid of North Korea, of war, of Communism, of all sorts of restrictions." Today, Il Soo Kim is married to a Korean woman, works for an airline, and enjoys his life in America. "I have much more in common with a native New Yorker than with a Korean greengrocer," he says.

The biggest changes for Korean immigrants, however, were still around the corner. As it turned out, things were going to go in unexpected directions. ▨

FESTIVALS AND CEREMONIES

What days are important in your life? Your birthday? Christmas? It's much the same with Koreans, but they have some interesting, different traditions.

Two Korean birthdays are celebrated the most: the first and the 60th. The first birthday of a child is called *Dol* and it is quite a celebration. All of the child's relatives come over in bright, colorful costumes, bringing lots of rice, cakes, cookies, and fruit. Everyone is there to wish this child a bright, happy, successful future. Many of the children there play a game called *yunnori*, a popular folk game that involves throwing four round-backed and flat-faced sticks into the air. Each child's score is then determined by how the sticks land.

The 60th birthday, on the other hand, is called *Hwankap*, and at this gathering, relatives are gathered together to celebrate the past rather than the future. Everyone looks back on the birthday person's accomplishments and successes and honors his or her long life.

For Koreans, March 1 is much like America's Fourth of July. They celebrate Independence Movement Day, when Korea broke free of Japan's unwanted control. July 17 is Constitution Day, celebrating when the country adopted the Republic of Korea Constitution in 1948, and October 3 is Korean Foundation Day, the anniversary of the founding of Korea as a nation by Tan-gun in 2333 B.C. Perhaps their biggest holiday is in September. *Chusok*, or Harvest Festival Day, is much like America's Thanksgiving. A feast is made, *ancestors* are remembered, and often there is a parade. It always falls at the time of the full moon and looking up at the moon is part of the ceremony. The actual Korean Thanksgiving is called *Chong-Gwon Park* and it is celebrated in cities like New York and Los Angeles with a festival. *Han-gul-nal,* or Korean Alphabet Day, is another holiday the Koreans enjoy. It celebrates the anniversary of when King Sejong created their unique alphabet in A.D. 1446.

Nine men in ceremonial costume celebrate Korea's Foundation Day on top of Mount Manisan. Foundation Day commemorates the establishment of Korea over 4,000 years ago.

부산
조방낙지
원조

간트호프

레스토랑

이방인

부대찌개
순 두 부
섞어찌개
낙지백반

삼 겹 살
돼지갈비
보   쌈
주 물 럭
곱창전골
낙지전골
조방낙지

부대찌개
섞어찌개
곱창전골

부낙순
대지두
찌복부
개음

4 Immigration Today

In 1965, something important happened that made all the difference for many immigrants. The Immigration Act that had restricted the number of Asians allowed to enter the United States was changed. Instead of limiting the numbers based on what country the immigrants were coming from, the new law based it on whether they met certain, specific requirements. The U.S. hoped that this would bring in educated and skilled workers to fill all the jobs that were now available in the booming economy. The idea worked, but not exactly as they had thought. Instead of receiving a flood of immigrants from Europe as they'd expected, a huge number of Koreans and other Asians came here instead. The Korean population grew at an incredible rate. Between 1970 and 1983, over 600,000 immigrants came to the United States. One of the reasons they didn't want to live in Korea anymore was that there was less and less room in which to live. Korea is a small country—about the size of the state of Maine—and yet it has more people than countries three and four times its size. There were far more people than there were

The bright lights of this Korean business district illuminate the way for pedestrians. Today, there are more than 15 million people of Asian descent living in the United States. Of that total, about 1.4 million are Korean American.

Former South Korean president Kim Young-sam waves to the public on the last day of his term in office. His election in 1987 marked an improvement in the quality of life for many South Koreans.

homes and jobs available, so they turned to a country where the people always seemed to have more than enough of everything—America.

In the meantime, the country was becoming increasingly aware of the Korean Americans' presence. In 1983, Congress passed a law that allowed **Amerasian** children of U.S. servicemen into the country, and then, in 1990, President George H. Bush declared May to be National Asian/Pacific-American Heritage Month.

Immigrants from Korea continue to come to the United States today. Most of them still live in large cities, such as Los Angeles, Chicago, and New York, but recently, they have started to move into areas of New Jersey (where the Korean American population has grown more than 200 percent since 1980) and other states. While through the 1980s and early 1990s Korean immigrants were coming into the U.S. at an average rate of about 30,000 a year, by the year 2008 the rate had fallen to around 17,000 annually. South Korea itself has changed quite a bit, with a better economy and more freedom. In 1987, Kim Young-sam was elected president of South Korea—the first one to be elected by the people in 16 years—and this has also meant fewer Koreans are leaving their homeland because they are no longer living under a *dictator*.

According to the 2006 American Community Survey, there are 1.3 million Korean Americans in the United States. The majority of them are second-generation Koreans over 60 years old; in other words, their parents were the ones to make the trip to the United States and they either came as small children or were born here soon after.

Emigrants from Korea are living in many countries other than the United States. In 2008, an estimated 3.7 million Korean immigrants were living in Canada, China, Japan, Russia, and the countries of Latin America.

In the U.S., 44 percent of Koreans live in the west, while 23 percent live in the northeast, 22 percent in the south, and 11 percent in the Midwest, according to the 2006 American Community Survey. The headquarters of most Korean-American organizations are still centered in Los Angeles, California. The Korean-American Museum, Korean Youth and Community Center, and the Korean Cultural Center are all located in Los Angeles, as is Koreatown, a 25-square-mile area that has over 3,500 prosperous Korean businesses and homes in it. Another Koreatown can be found in Flushing, New York. Both New York and Los Angeles offer several Korean daily newspapers, with most of the articles coming out of Seoul, Korea, as well as special sections devoted to the concerns and activities of the different Korean groups within the United States. There are also several television and radio stations in these cities with all-Korean programs and news from the Korean Broadcasting Station in Seoul.

Members of the South Korean military guard the eastern border of the Republic of Korea. North Korea is still ruled by a Communist dictatorship, and has been the target of economic sanctions by the United States and other countries because of its rulers' programs to develop nuclear weapons.

If you were in a completely different country, far from your family and the things you were familiar with, would you want to spend a lot of time with others who understood you, your language,

A South Korean woman burns incense and prays for peace and prosperity at a Buddhist temple during the Lunar New Year. The holiday is important to the Korean culture—much like the New Year people traditionally celebrate in America.

and how you feel? Korean Americans definitely feel that way and, since they first started arriving in 1902, have created many Korean churches and other organizations. There are Korean business associations, sports groups, and political organizations that help bring Koreans together to talk, share information, and make friends. These gatherings help the immigrants' children learn how to speak and understand Korean and often helps to show them some of the most important Korean traditions and activities. They are also a way for the first-generation Koreans to share their heritage with their second-generation children, which, hopefully, will continue to be passed down through the ages so it is never lost.

Like all the other people who have come here from other countries, Korean Americans have contributed to making this country more interesting and *diverse*. In searching for a better life, Korean immigrants have, in turn, enriched this country, too. ◼

The first wave of Korean immigrants came here to work on pineapple and sugar plantations, but after they finished—or quit—working on the plantations, many of the immigrants either went to live in Honolulu or on the mainland. There, they opened their own stores, bathhouses, and boarding houses. Others went to California where they worked as migrant farm workers, cooks, railroad section hands, and domestic servants (maids, butlers, gardeners, and so on).

This strip mall in Los Angeles is full of Korean businesses, including doctors, dentists, and grocery stores. Large cities have areas known as Koreatowns, where people can buy imported Korean products and maintain a connection with their homeland.

Because education is so important to Korean families, the parents would often work hard so that their children would have the opportunity to have better educations and better-paying jobs in the future.

A number of Korean immigrants came to North America as professionals in the medical field, and that is how they are still working today. Most of the other Korean Americans either own their own businesses or work for other Korean employers. Some of the common businesses Korean Americans choose to open are liquor stores, nail salons, dry cleaners, and photo stores. Some of them invested in *garment* factories, selling bags, hats, and other clothing. A great many Koreans living in the big cities run their own *greengroceries*, or fresh fruit and vegetable markets. There are currently more than 1,400 Korean greengrocers just in New York City. It does not take a great deal of money to start these businesses, and it is easy work to learn. Running a greengrocery also means the Koreans don't have to have a good command of the English language, something that is required in many other jobs. Often, the entire family works at the store, from children to grandparents, and they work hard, usually up to 16 hours a day, or 112 hours a week, without a single vacation.

In the last few decades, more than half of the people coming to the United States from Korea were women. At first, most of these women were the wives of U.S. servicemen, but more recently the number of other women has increased. For women one of the main differences between life in Korea and life in the United States is that in Korea, once they are married, a

A selection of vegetables is displayed in a Korean street market. Many Korean Americans have become successful by opening small grocery stories in the United States or Canada.

KOREAN STORYTELLING

Have you ever stood up and told a story or sung a song to a bunch of friends or family? Can you imagine doing it when you're just getting over a cold and your voice is still hoarse? This is what happens in Korea. They have a tradition called *P'ansori*, which means "song on a large flat area where people gather together." Performers who know how to do this must work very hard. They sing their stories to the audience, and some stories can last as long as eight hours! The songs are not soft and smooth, however, instead they are rough and raspy. The composers try to imitate the sounds of nature when they write these songs. Performers must train for years to wear down their vocal cords enough so that they sound hoarse all the time. In the past, they did this by standing under a waterfall and screaming until their voices gave out. Performers must also memorize the story, which can be difficult when it is so long.

P'ansori performers can be men or women. On stage, they carry a fan and move around as they sing. The only instrument they have to accompany them is a drum called a *puk*. You can sometimes see these performers in theatres and concerts in large cities; one of the masters of the *p'ansori* is a woman called Yoojin Chung, who currently lives in the state of Washington.

woman's main responsibilities are within the home, doing housework and taking care of the children. Over two-thirds of the women in Korea do not have any type of job outside the home. In the U.S., on the other hand, more than 70 percent of the married Korean women work outside the home, usually in family businesses as cashiers or sales clerks. In recent years, some of these women have even opened up their own businesses.

Korean businesses almost always do well thanks to the hard work and long hours Korean Americans are willing to put into

A man reads a Korean newspaper in a park in Los Angeles. Korean-language movies, books, and newspapers help keep immigrants in touch with their culture and their native country.

A Korean man stands in front of his looted and fire-gutted store several days after the Los Angeles riots of 1992. Rioters were reacting to the verdict in the Rodney King trial, in which four white L.A. police officers were found not guilty of assault for beating a black motorist outside the city. During the three-day spree by angry protesters, over 5,270 buildings had been destroyed or damaged. Unfortunately, riots centered on an area of the city that included many Korean-owned businesses, and innocent shopkeepers suffered as a result.

them. There's another reason they do well, however—they frequently have the finances available that they need to succeed. First of all, most immigrants sell off most of what they have before leaving the country. This can often result in a good amount of money to start over with again in America. Before 1978, immigrants were only allowed to bring in $1,000 with them, but by 1990, this figure had been raised to $200,000. Second, it isn't unusual for relatives of the immigrants to donate their own extra money to help with the new venture. Third, the Koreans have a private banking system called *kae*. Within this system, other Korean Americans donate money for grants and loans to help new Korean businesses get started.

In April 1992, however, there was a tragedy that no amount of money could have prevented. The Koreans call it *sa-i-ku*, which means April 29th. Angered by a **verdict** in an important trial (the Rodney King case), **looters** began to riot in inner city Los Angeles. They burned, destroyed, and damaged over 2,500 Korean businesses. Eight out of every 10 Korean stores were attacked, and there was over $350 million in losses. All over the United States, Koreans gathered together and created fundraisers of all kinds to help raise money for these families. They were able to raise an amazing $4.5 million for the victims.

Despite this setback, Korean Americans continue to prosper in their new country. Their hard work and determination has made them among the most successful people to come to North America. ✹

Famous Korean Americans

Ahn Ik-t'ae

Ahn (1906–1965) was a Korean composer who lived in Philadelphia. He wrote the Korean national anthem in 1936.

Philip Ahn

Ahn (1905–1978)was born in Los Angeles, California, the son of one of Korea's best-known freedom fighters, Do San. He grew up to become one of the world's most recognized Asian-American actors, starring in well over 100 movies with such stars as Elvis Presley, John Wayne, Gary Cooper, and Shirley Temple. He was most well known for his role as Master Kan in the 1970s television series *Kung Fu*.

Sarah Chang

Chang (b. 1980) is the daughter of Korean immigrants who came to the United States in 1979. When she was only five years old, she began performing on her violin, and within a year, she was taking classes at the famous Julliard School of Music in New York City. She has had many memorable performances, and through 2008 had recorded 17 albums.

Channing Liem

A diplomat, scholar, and minister, Channing (1909–1996) received his college degrees in the United States and then became pastor of the New York City Korean Church, the only Korean church in the country at that time.

Margaret Cho

Margaret is a comedian and in 1994 became the first Korean American to star in her own television show, called "All-American Girl." Her reality TV show, *The Cho Show*, debuted on VH1 in August 2008.

Sara Choe

Choe was the first of the 1,000 picture brides that came to the United States from Korea between 1910 and 1924.

Judge Herbert Choy

In 1971, Choy (1916–2004) became the first Asian American to be appointed to the United States federal court. He served until 1984.

Eugene Chung

In1992, Chung became the first Korean American to be drafted in the first round of the NFL draft. He played five seasons of professional football.

Halla Pai Huhm

Huhm (1922–1994) was known and respected for teaching Korean dance to many people in the United States. She taught at the University of Hawaii's Manoa campus and in 1950, she opened her own Korean dance studio. In 1980, she received the cultural medal from South Korea—the first person not living in Korea to do so.

Philip Jaisohn

Born Suh Jae-pil, Jaisohn (1864–1951)was the first Korean to become an naturalized American citizen (1885) and the first to receive an American medical degree (1892). In 1896, he returned to Korea and established the first Korean newspaper.

Kim Chong-nim

Known as the Rice King, he was a successful Korean-American rice farmer who donated three planes to the new School of Aviation in 1919.

Charles Kim (Kim Ho) and Harry Kim (Kim Hyung-soon)

These brothers established Kim Brothers Company in California, where they became famous for creating new types of fruit, including the nectarine.

Jay Kim

In 1992, Kim became the first Korean American to be elected to Congress.

Sammy Lee

Lee was born in 1920 to Korean immigrants who were working on a Hawaiian plantation. He was the first Asian American to win an Olympic gold medal for the 10-meter platform in the 1948 Olympics in London. In 1952, he won another Olympic gold medal for the 10-meter and a bronze medal for the three-meter springboard in Helsinki. He was later elected to the International Swimming Hall of Fame and the U.S. Olympic Hall of Fame and has been a swimming coach to the U.S. diving teams going to the Olympic games. Today, he is a physician and father of two.

Syngman Rhee

Rhee (1875–1965) was a man determined to fight for his country's freedom. He was in prison from 1897 until 1904 for political reasons and when he was released, he came to the U.S. to try and convince President Theodore Roosevelt to protect Korea from the Japanese. Roosevelt refused, but Rhee stayed in this country for the next 40 years, getting three different college degrees and writing his book, The Spirit of Independence. At the end of World War II, he returned to Korea and became the first President of the Republic of Korea in 1948. In 1960, he was forced into exile and he lived the rest of his life in the United States.

Do San

Also known as Ahn Chang-Ho, San (1878–1938) spent 23 years of his life fighting for independence for Korea. He helped to establish the first private, modern school in Korea, and in 1902, he came to the U.S. and formed the Korean National Association. He returned to Korea a few years later and toured the nation warning the people of the coming invasion by the Japanese. In 1932, the Japanese imprisoned him and he died just after being released in 1938.

Immigration Figures

Korean Immigrants Obtaining U.S. Citizenship, by Decade

1940-49:	**83**
1950-59:	**4,845**
1960-69:	**27,048**
1970-79:	**241,192**
1980-89:	**322,708**
1990-99:	**179,770**
2000-07	**158,021**

No data available before 1940.

Source: Yearbook of Immigration Statistics, 2007.

Glossary

Amerasian a person who has one Asian parent and one American parent.

Ancestors members of a family who lived a long time ago.

Armistice a temporary agreement to stop fighting a war.

Ban a legal or formal prohibition of something.

Dictator a person who has complete control over a country, usually ruling it unfairly.

Diverse composed of distinct qualities.

Exile a person who has been forced out of his or her country and ordered not to return.

Famine a serious lack of food.

Garment a piece of clothing.

Greengrocery a fresh fruit and vegetable market, often located outdoors.

Immigrant a person who comes from abroad to live permanently in another country.

Looter a person who steals from stores or homes during a riot or war.

Philosopher a person who studies philosophy, which is the study of truth, wisdom, the nature of reality, and knowledge.

Romanization the process of using letters to write out words that are usually written in symbols.

Shortage not enough of something, a lack.

Verdict the decision of a jury as to whether a person is guilty or not guilty, or a decision or opinion on something.

Further Reading

Books

Balgassi, Haemi. *Tae's Sonata.* New York: Clarion Books, 1997.

Bercaw, Edna Coe. *Halmoni's Day.* New York: Dial Books for Young Readers, 2000.

Cieslik, Thomas, et al, editors. *Immigration: A Documentary and Reference Guide.* Westport, Conn.: Greenhaven Press, 2008.

Kim, Patti. *A Cab Called Reliable.* New York: St. Martin's Press, Inc., 1998.

Kim, Robert and Ruth Turk. *I Am Korean-American (Our American Family).* New York: Powerkids' Press, 1998.

O'Donnell. *U.S. Immigration.* Mankato, Minn.: Capstone Press, 2008.

Finding Your Korean-American Ancestors

Byers, Paula K., ed. *Asian American Genealogical Sourcebook.* Detroit: Gale Research, 1995.

Carmack, Sharon DeBartolo. *A Genealogist's Guide to Discovering Your Immigrant and Ethnic Ancestors.* Cincinnati: Betterway Books, 2000.

Internet Resources

http://www.ooncuc.gov

The official Web site of the U.S. Bureau of the Census contains information about the most recent census taken in 2000.

http://www12.statcan.ca/english/census/index.cfm

The Web site for Canada's Bureau of Statistics, which includes population information updated for the most recent census in May 2006.

http://www.askasia.org/

This Web site provides information for K-12 educators and students interested in Asian and Asian American studies.

http://www.hkccweb.org/en/

The Hawaii Korean Chamber of Commerce works to enrich the lives and businesses of Korean Americans in Hawaii, as well as encourage goodwill among Korean Americans and their communities and abroad.

http://www.kahs.org/

This Web site seeks to continually develop and maintain the heritage of Korean Americans within the United States and the global community.

http://www.kamuseum.org/

This is the Web site of the Korean-American Museum, which promotes Korean American history and culture, as well as recognizing Korean contributions to America.

Index

Photo Credits

Contributors

Barry Moreno has been librarian and historian at the Ellis Island Immigration Museum and the Statue of Liberty National Monument since 1988. He is the author of *The Statue of Liberty Encyclopedia,* which was published by Simon & Schuster in October 2000. He is a native of Los Angeles, California. After graduation from California State University at Los Angeles, where he earned a degree in history, he joined the National Park Service as a seasonal park ranger at the Statue of Liberty; he eventually became the monument's librarian. In his spare time, Barry enjoys reading, writing, and studying foreign languages and grammar. His biography has been included in *Who's Who Among Hispanic Americans, The Directory of National Park Service Historians, Who's Who in America,* and *The Directory of American Scholars.*

Tamra Orr is a professional writer living in Indiana. She is the author of two books and writes for a large variety of national magazines. She has been married for 19 years, and she and her husband home-school their four children, ages 17 to 5. Both of them admit that their kids teach them something new every day.